Audubon's Plate 26 Carolina Parrot

Classic Designs Cross Stitch Pattern

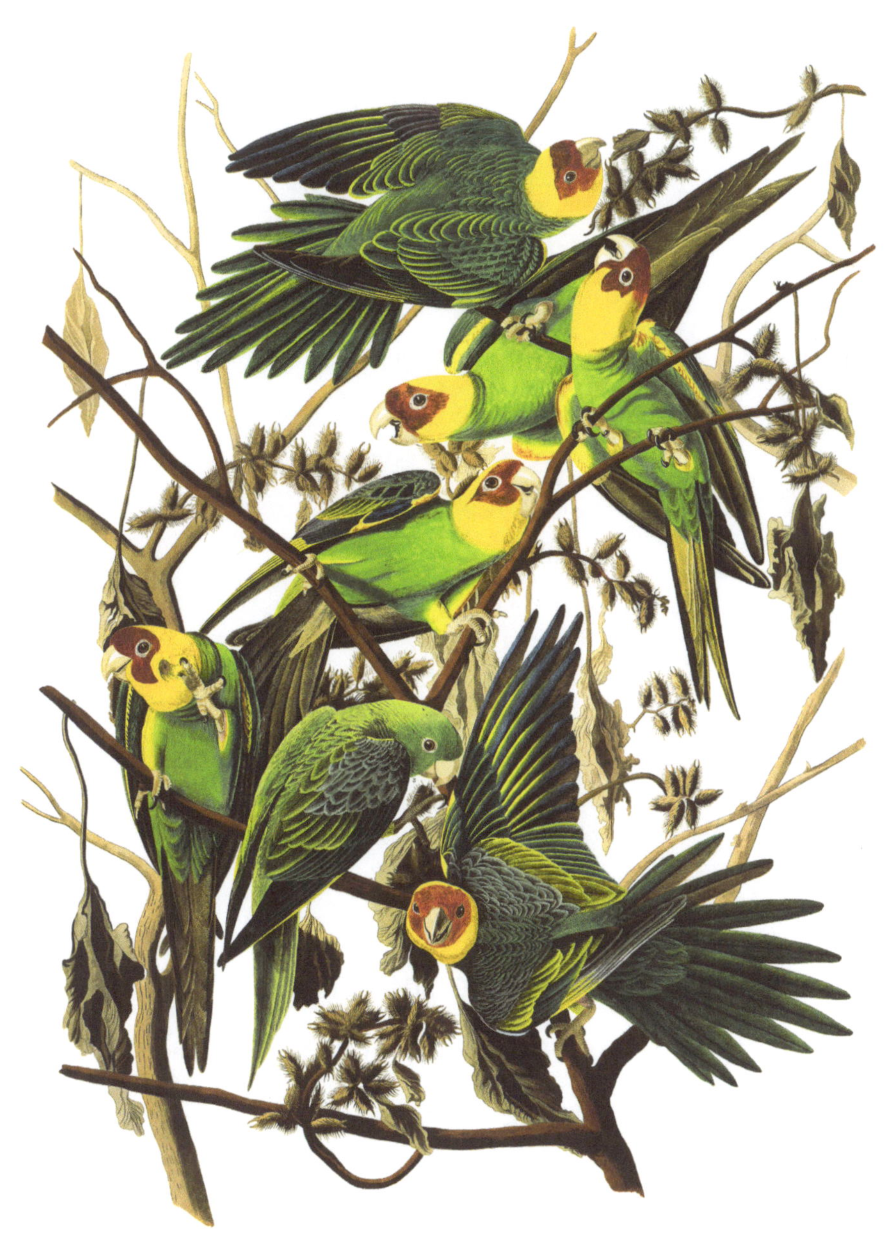

M. Norah Halsey

ISBN-10: 1-64004-275-X

ISBN-13: 978-1-64004-275-9

Designs by Norah
A Division of Silver City Publications
P.O. Box 1914
Nampa, ID 83653

Basic Cross Stitch Instructions

Determine Center of Fabric & Graph: Fold the fabric in half from side to side and from bottom to top. Use a needle or thread to mark the center in the folded corner. Count from the center of the fabric to the place you wish to start on the graph. The center of the graph is designated by I which point to the center of the grid. Each square on the graph represents a square on the fabric.

Number of Strands of Floss & Needle size chart:

Fabric Ct.	Cross Stitch	Backstitch	Needle Size
5-6	6	3	22
7-9	4	2	24
10-13	3	2	24
14-19	2	1	24
20+	1	1	26

*Stitched over One Thread

Stitch Over 1 Thread

Floss: To stitch, pull one strand and separate the given number of strands from the 6 strand twist. Pull one at a time to avoid tangles. Use 2 strands for cross stitch and ½ stitch, and use 1 strand for backstitch unless instructed.

Cross stitch: The cross stitch is the basic stitch, where an X is formed by crossing over an intersection of two threads. When you begin the first stitch, leave a tail of approximately 1 inch of floss on the back of the fabric. This excess floss will be tacked down by the first few stitches. Do not use a knot to secure the fabric as this will cause lumps in the back of the piece.

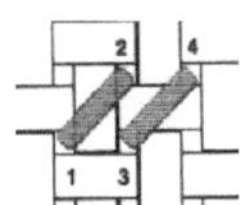

To start a cross stitch pattern:
Come up through hole 1 and back through hole 2.
Come up through hole 3 and go back through hole 4.

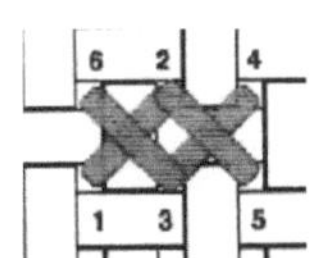

To complete the stitches:
Come up through hole 5 and back through hole 2.
Come up through hole 3 and back through hole 6.

If one color runs consecutively, all bottom halves of the cross stitch pattern can be worked in one direction and the top halves worked when coming back. The top thread should always lie in the same direction.

Backstitch: A backstitch is used to outline make lines and is often used to form letters. Come up at 1 and back through 2 to make the first stitch. Come up through 3 and down through 1 to make the 2nd stitch. Go up through 4 and down through 3 to make the third stitch. After the 1st stitch, all other stitches are formed by looping back on top and then coming up ahead of the next stitch.

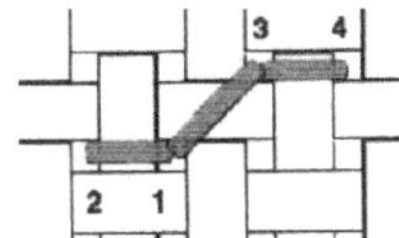

Long Stitch: A long stitch is similar to a back stitch, but can be longer and may not be confined to a diagonal. On the graph come up at one end of the line and down at the other.

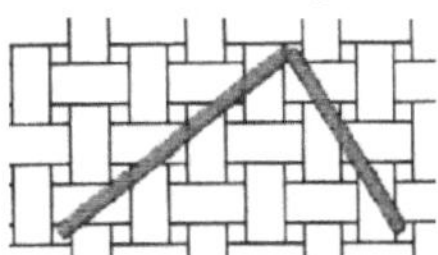

1/2 Stitch: The ½ stitch is the first half of the full cross stitch or 1 diagonal. See the "to start a cross stitch pattern" diagram. In this diagram, the image is designed from lower left to upper right.

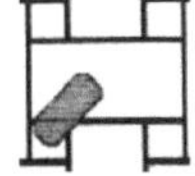

1/4 Stitch: The ¼ stitch is made with a half diagonal.

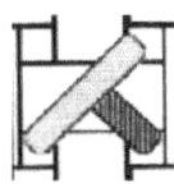

3/4 Stitch: A ¾ stitch is made with a complete diagonal and a half diagonal. The complete diagonal is done in the direction of the slash in the square of the design graph and the half diagonal is done on the side containing the symbol.

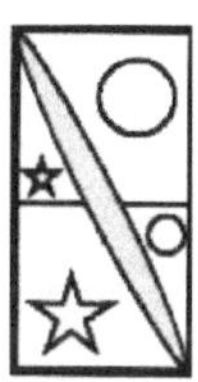

2 symbols in 1 square: If 2 symbol colors are in the same square, the symbol color closest to you is the dominant color and will be a ¾ stitch and the other symbol color will be the ¼ stitch. It will be necessary to stitch the ¾ and ¼ stitch to cover the fabric sufficiently.

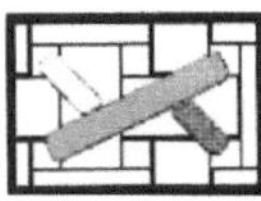

Special Shaping Stitch: A special shaping stitch is used to create gentle sloping lines. It consists of a long stitch and 1 or 2 quarter stitches. The ¼ stitch is done in the color indicated by the symbol in that square. Note: When working with 14 count fabric, the ¼ stitches may not cover the fabric sufficiently. If this is the case, use a ¾ stitch and a ¼ stitch on each side of the long stitch.

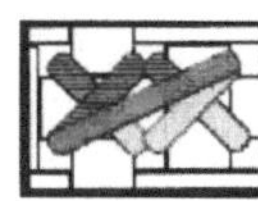

Stitch Over 2 Threads

Cross stitch: Come up at 1 and instead of going down in the hole diagonally across, go one more diagonal to 2. The diagonal is 2s squares long. Come up at 3 and repeat the above step. Go down at 4 and then come up at 5. Go back through hole, come up through hole 3, and then go back through hole 6. Note there are empty holes between each of the legs of the X and an empty hole in the center. Four squares are covered. If one color runs consecutively, work all the bottom diagonals in the same row and work across coming back.

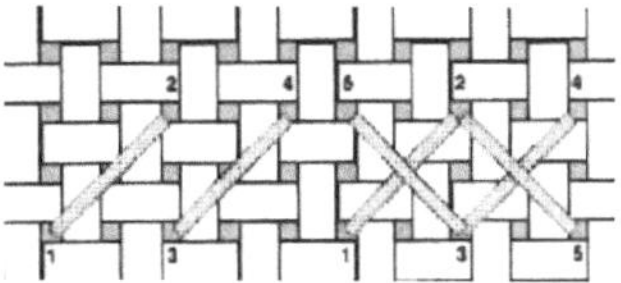

Backstitch: The backstitch will also go over 2 squares in the diagonal, vertical, or horizontal.

Other stitches: The other stitches are done the same as when using 2 threads. Note that 1 square on the graph is equivalent to 2 threads on the fabric.

Basic Cross Stitch Instructions

Couching Stitch: A couching stitch is a technique where a thread is laid over fabric and then attached to it with an additional thread sewn over it. Lay the thread down along the designated line as shown on the graph and with the matching thread, come up at A and go down at B wrapping a small, tight stich over the lid thread at regular intervals as shown. Finally, secure the thread in the back.

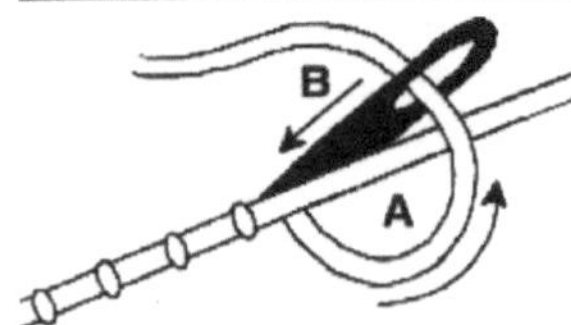

French Knot: Insert the needle where indicated on the chart. Hold the thread taut and start at the base of the working thread, wrap the thread around the needle, spiraling away from the fabric as many times as indicated on the instruction chart. Turn the needle and reinsert it at the next fabric thread. Pull the needle on through while holding the wrapped threads flat against the fabric.

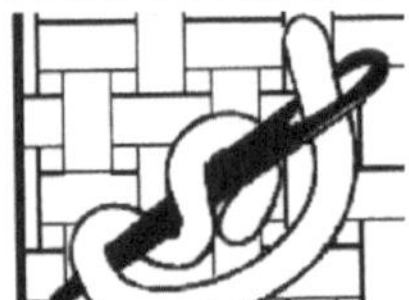

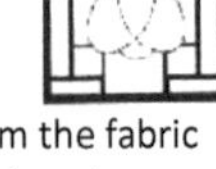

Attaching Beads: Use a beading needle and come up through the bottom left hold of the square, thread on a bead and go down through the upper right hole of your square. Loop through once more to secure your bead.

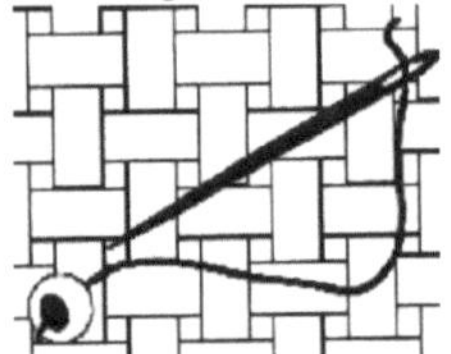

Finishing

Washing and Pressing: Use dishwashing liquid in lukewarm water. Soak the stitchery and swish gently and then rinse completely in lukewarm water. Roll the stitchery in a clean towel and squeeze. Place a double layer of towels on an ironing board. Place the stitchery face down on the towels. Set the iron to a cotton setting and press until the fabric and stitchery are completely dry. Note: Vinegar in the wash water will help prevent certain color threads from running.

Loose threads on back of work: Do not jump too far from one area to another, instead finish off and start again. Loose threads, particularly dark colors will show through on the front.

General Tips

Avoid fabric reveling: You can stitch around the edges with thread, or cut fabric one inch larger than needed and tape the edges with a fold of masking tape. The tape can be cut off when completed.

Place fabric in a hoop: Gently pull the fabric taut and tighten the screw. The screw should be in the ten-o-clock position if you are right handed and at the one-o-clock position if you are left handed. This will prevent the floss from becoming tangled in the screw with each stitch.

Do not knot thread: As mentioned earlier do not knot the thread behind the fabric to secure it by the first two or three stitches made. A knot will make a bumpy back surface and the work will not lay flat when completed.

Use the stab-stick method: Avoid pulling the fabric out of shape. The stab-stick method is done in 2 motions, straight up and straight down, while keeping the fabric taut. Do not pull the thread taut just pull it snug. This method will ensure the thread lies just where you want it and will not be pulled too tightly, thereby pulling the fabric out of shape.

Finish all threads: run the needle under four or more stitches on the back of the design and cut close. To begin a new thread, run needle under several stitches and catch the end of the thread.

Twisted thread: If the thread becomes twisted, just drop the needle and let it hang down. It will unwind by itself. The floss appears thinner as it twists and will not cover well, so avoid using stitching with a twisted thread.

Needles: Do not leave a needle in the design area of the work as it may rust over time.

Soak in water before assembling: Soak the completed design in cold water before assembling. Press with a warm iron on the reverse side.

Fabric: Aida 14, White
112w X 136h Stitches

Strands: 2
Type: DMC

18 Count Aida:

Stitch Area: 12 1/2w x 15 1/4h inches or 31.6w x 38.4h cm

Fabric Size with 2-inch (5 cm) margin: 16w x 19h inches or 42w x 49h cm

16 Count Aida:

Stitch Area: 14w x 17h inches or 35.6w x 43.2h cm

Fabric Size with 2-inch (5 cm) margin: 18w x 21h inches or 46w x 53h cm

14 Count Aida:

Stitch Area: approx. 16w x 19 1/2h inches or 40.6w x 49.3h cm

Fabric Size with 2-inch (5 cm) margin: 20w x 23h inches or 51w x 60h cm

Floss Used for Full Stitches:

	Symbol	Number	Color
	ϐ	165	Moss Green-VY LT
	⅃	166	Moss Green-MD LT
	//	167	Yellow Beige-VY DK
	➔	221	Shell Pink-VY DK
	|	225	Shell Pink-UL VY LT
	✱	301	Mahogany-MD
	■	310	Black
	⊞	318	Steel Gray-LT
	◪	355	Terra Cotta-DK
	⌖	370	Mustard-MD
	⁚	371	Mustard
	Ⅱ	372	Mustard-LT
	◓	400	Mahogany-DK
	∩	407	Desert Sand-DK
	✪	413	Pewter Gray-DK
	⊥	414	Steel Gray-DK
	⟁	420	Hazelnut Brown-DK
	⋈	422	Hazelnut Brown-LT
	◖	433	Brown-MD
	●	434	Brown-LT
	z	435	Brown-VY LT

	Symbol	Number	Color
	#	436	Tan
	∷	437	Tan-LT
	∴	451	Shell Gray-DK
	••	452	Shell Gray-MD
	⬯	453	Shell Gray-LT
	◘	469	Avocado Green
	❀	470	Avocado Green-LT
	%	471	Avocado Green-VY LT
	√	472	Avocado Green-UL LT
	✖	498	Christmas Red-DK
	●	500	Blue Green-VY DK
	⬮	520	Fern Green-DK
	⊁	524	Fern Green-VY LT
	▩	535	Ash Gray-VY LT
	∟	543	Beige Brown-UL VY LT
	✣	580	Moss Green-DK
	◉	581	Moss Green
	✚	610	Drab Brown-DK
	⤧	611	Drab Brown
	⋙	612	Drab Brown-LT
	~	613	Drab Brown-VY LT
	⊛	632	Desert Sand-UL VY DK
	⌶	640	Beige Gray-VY DK
	$	642	Beige Gray-DK
	5	644	Beige Gray-MD
	◤	645	Beaver Gray-VY DK
	⋋	646	Beaver Gray-DK
	ž	647	Beaver Gray-MD
	+	648	Beaver Gray-LT
	◊	676	Old Gold-LT
	:	677	Old Gold-VY LT
	♧	680	Old Gold-DK
	€	704	Chartreuse-BRT
	○	712	Cream
	4	725	Topaz
	–	728	Topaz
	H	729	Old Gold-MD
	⊂	730	Olive Green-VY DK
	◣	731	Olive Green-DK
	✷	732	Olive Green
	▣	733	Olive Green-MD
	中	734	Olive Green-LT
	⊠	738	Tan-VY LT
	▷	739	Tan-UL VY LT
	☆	742	Tangerine-LT
	I	743	Yellow-MD
	·	744	Yellow-Pale
	·|·	758	Terra Cotta-VY LT
	<	762	Pearl Gray-VY LT
	↓	779	Cocoa-DK
	◖	780	Topaz-UL VY DK

	Symbol	Number	Color
	✦	781	Topaz-VY DK
	L	782	Topaz-DK
	☘	783	Topaz-MD
	8	801	Coffee Brown-DK
	⭘	814	Garnet-DK
	⬮	815	Garnet-MD
	∞	819	Baby Pink-LT
	^	822	Beige Gray-LT
	♣	829	Golden Olive-VY DK
	∩	830	Golden Olive-DK
	◆◆	831	Golden Olive-MD
	‹	832	Golden Olive
	#	833	Golden Olive-LT
	⬁	834	Golden Olive-VY LT
	⊘	838	Beige Brown-VY DK
	▲	839	Beige Brown-DK
	★	840	Beige Brown-MD
	✕	841	Beige Brown-LT
	◱	842	Beige Brown-VY LT
	▼	844	Beaver Brown-UL DK
	♠	869	Hazelnut Brown-VY DK
	⚓	898	Coffee Brown-VY DK
	✿	902	Garnet-VY DK
	◈	907	Parrot Green-LT
	↘	918	Red Copper-DK
	◒	919	Red Copper
	◀	920	Copper-MD
	/	928	Gray Green-VY LT
	⬢	934	Black Avocado Green
	⬆	935	Avocado Green-DK
	✤	936	Avocado Green-VY DK
	ɸ	937	Avocado Green-MD
	❽	938	Coffee Brown-UL DK
	0	945	Tawny
	0	948	Peach-VY LT
	6	950	Desert Sand-LT
	(	951	Tawny-LT
	✚	975	Golden Brown-DK
	⧖	976	Golden Brown-MD
	⚘	987	Forest Green-DK
	o	3011	Khaki Green-DK
	↘	3012	Khaki Green-MD
	×	3013	Khaki Green-LT
	⧗	3021	Brown Gray-VY DK
	⊕	3022	Brown Gray-MD
	✓	3023	Brown Gray-LT
	9	3024	Brown Gray-VY LT
	♥	3031	Mocha Brown-VY DK
	⊙	3032	Mocha Brown-MD
	♡	3033	Mocha Brown-VY LT

Symbol	Number	Color
=	3042	Antique Violet-LT
ȡ	3045	Yellow Beige-DK
7	3046	Yellow Beige-MD
±	3047	Yellow Beige-LT
▨	3051	Green Gray-DK
⌖	3052	Green Gray-MD
◎	3053	Green Gray
ʌ	3064	Desert Sand
)	3072	Beaver Gray-VY LT
☽	3346	Hunter Green
✳	3347	Yellow Green-MD
•	3348	Yellow Green-LT
✽	3362	Pine Green-DK
❖	3363	Pine Green-MD
•	3364	Pine Green
◘	3371	Black Brown
◪	3721	Shell Pink-DK
3	3743	Antique Violet-VY LT
∾	3756	Baby Blue-UL VY LT
n	3770	Tawny-VY LT
◈	3772	Desert Sand-VY DK
ž	3773	Desert Sand-MD
0	3774	Desert Sand-VY LT
⬅	3777	Terra Cotta-VY DK
e	3779	Terra Cotta-UL VY LT
✝	3781	Mocha Brown-DK
2	3782	Mocha Brown-LT
⁂	3787	Brown Gray-DK
❃	3790	Beige Gray-UL DK
◆	3799	Pewter Gray-VY DK
⟠	3819	Moss Green-LT
↑	3820	Straw-DK
⋘	3821	Straw
⇦	3822	Straw-LT
	3823	Yellow-UL Pale
↖	3828	Hazelnut Brown
◂	3829	Old Gold-VY DK
木	3830	Terra Cotta-MD
T	3852	Straw-VY DK
⇨	3855	Autumn Gold-LT
⬓	3857	Rosewood-DK
⍁	3859	Rosewood-LT
☼	3860	Cocoa
ǂ	3861	Cocoa-LT
═	3862	Mocha Beige-DK
⫽	3863	Mocha Beige-MD
❍	3864	Mocha Beige-LT
«	3865	Winter White
∘	3866	Mocha Brown-UL VY LT
1	B5200	Snow White

Floss Notes

Floss Notes

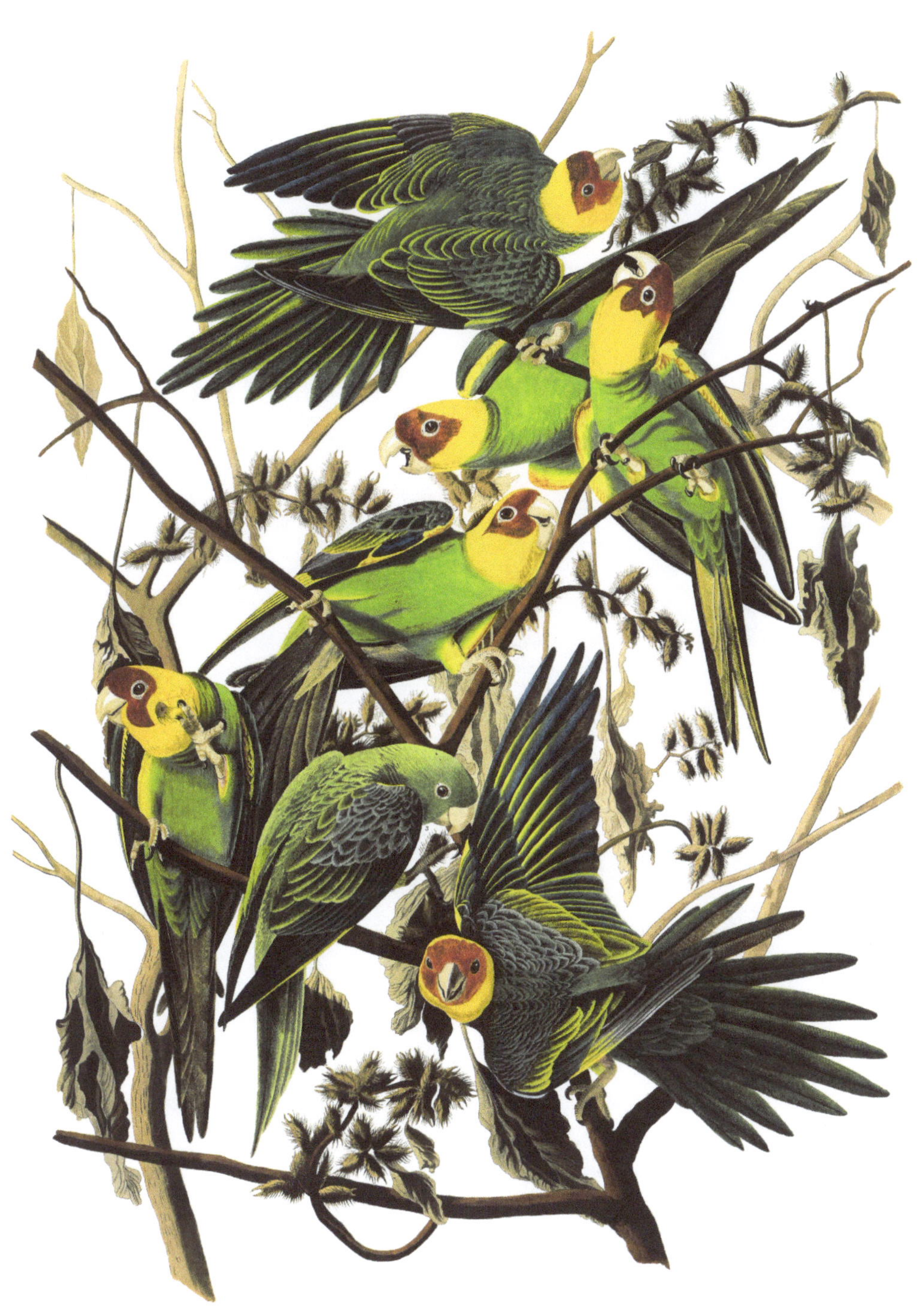

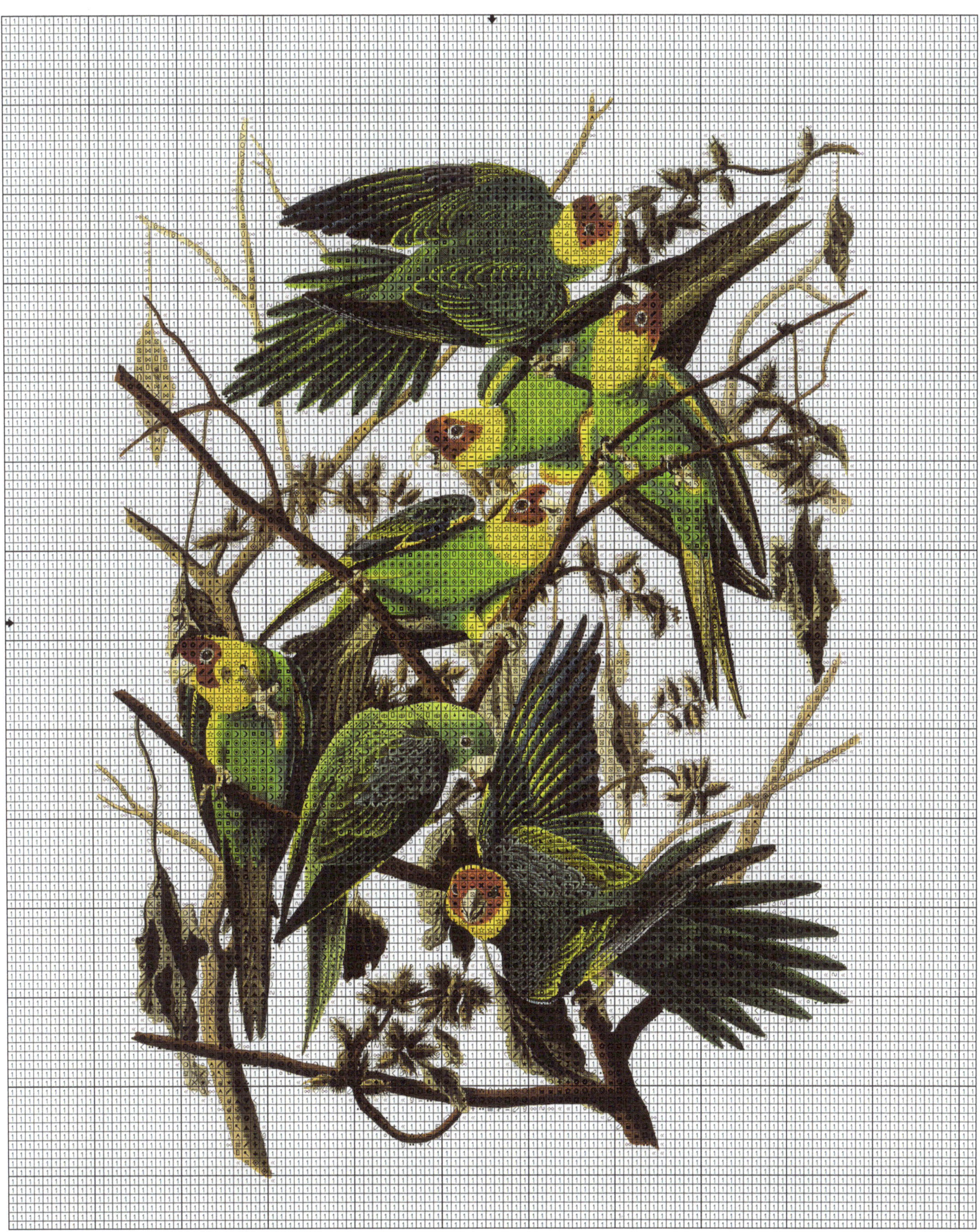

Quadrant Map

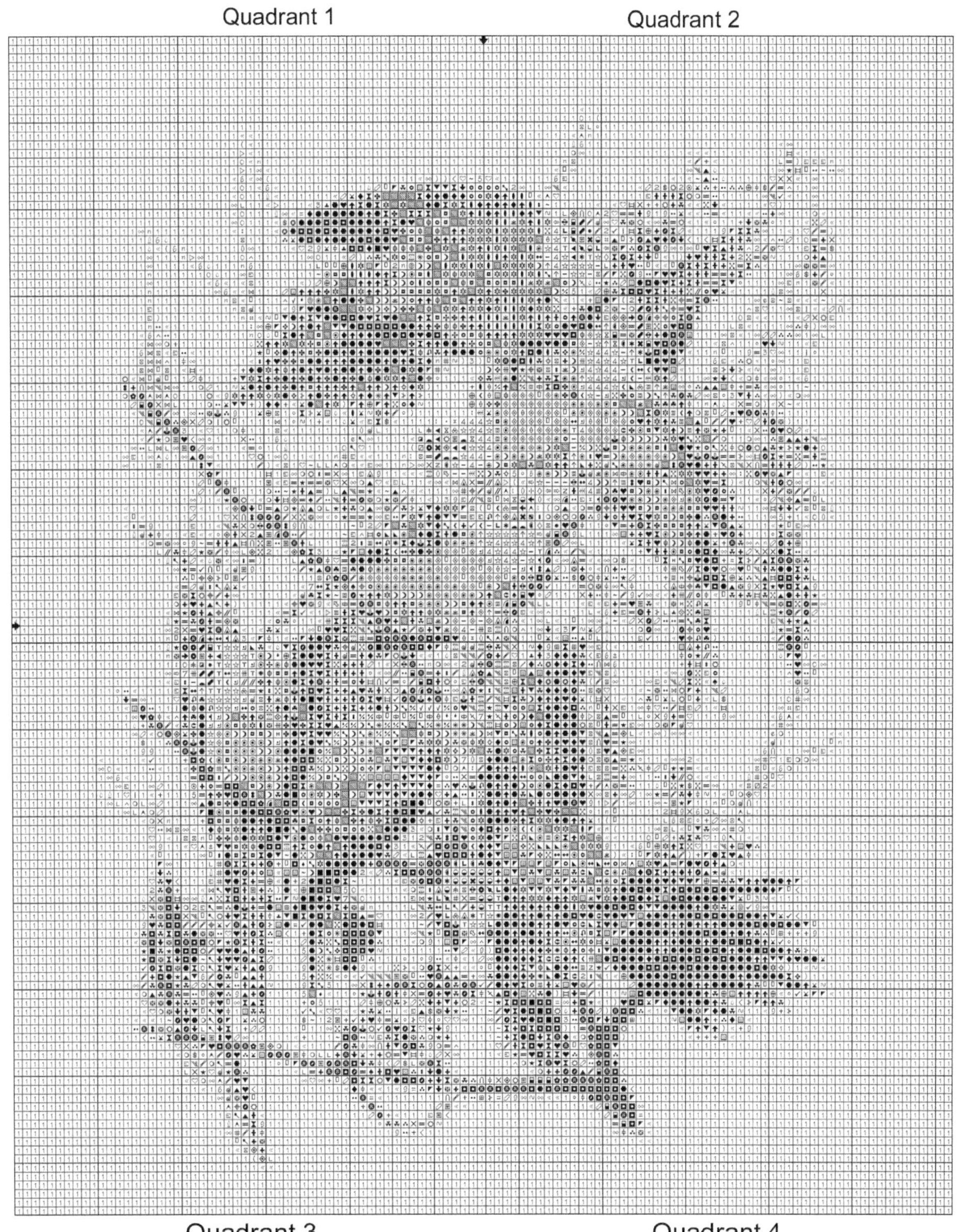

Quadrant 1

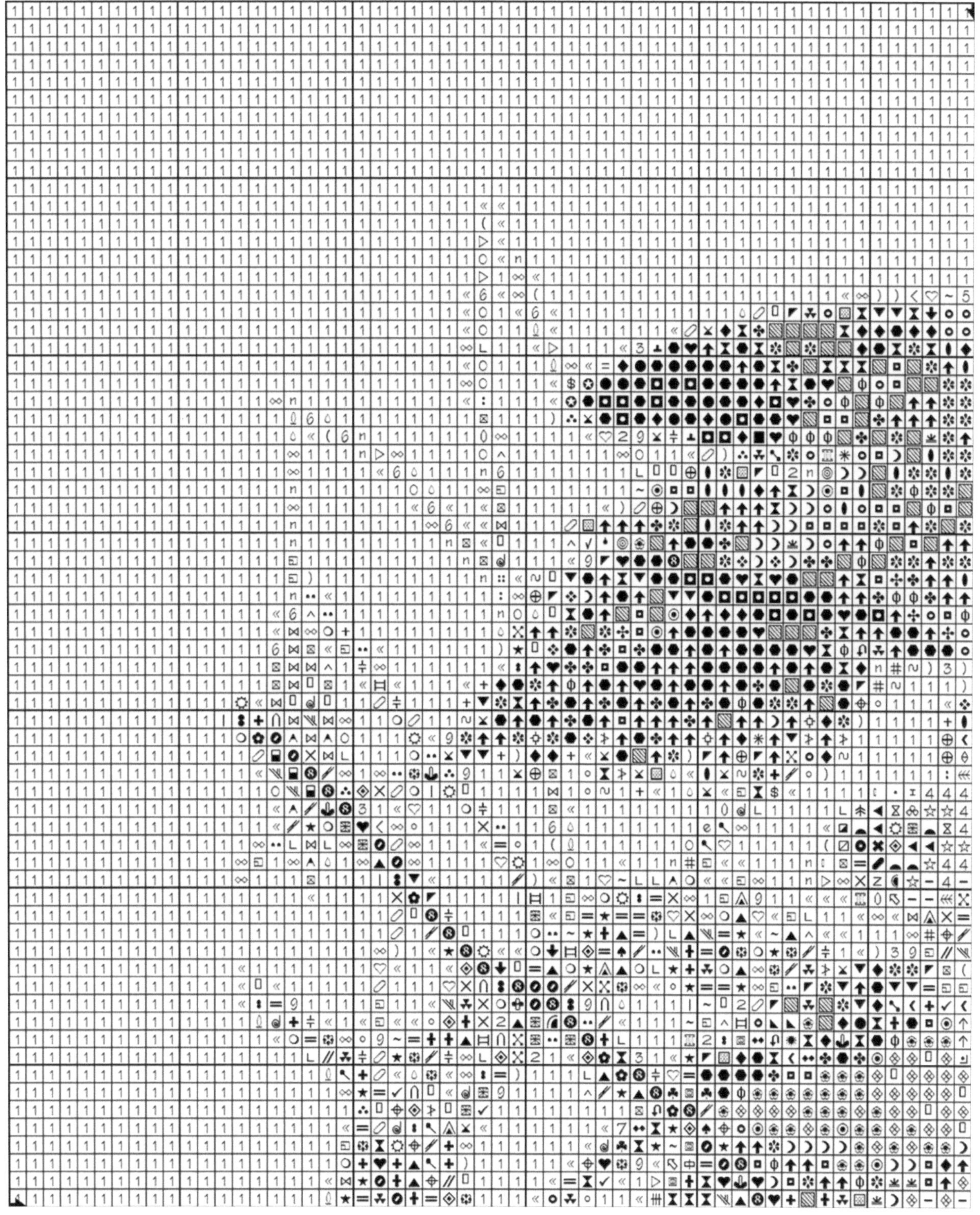

Quadrant 2

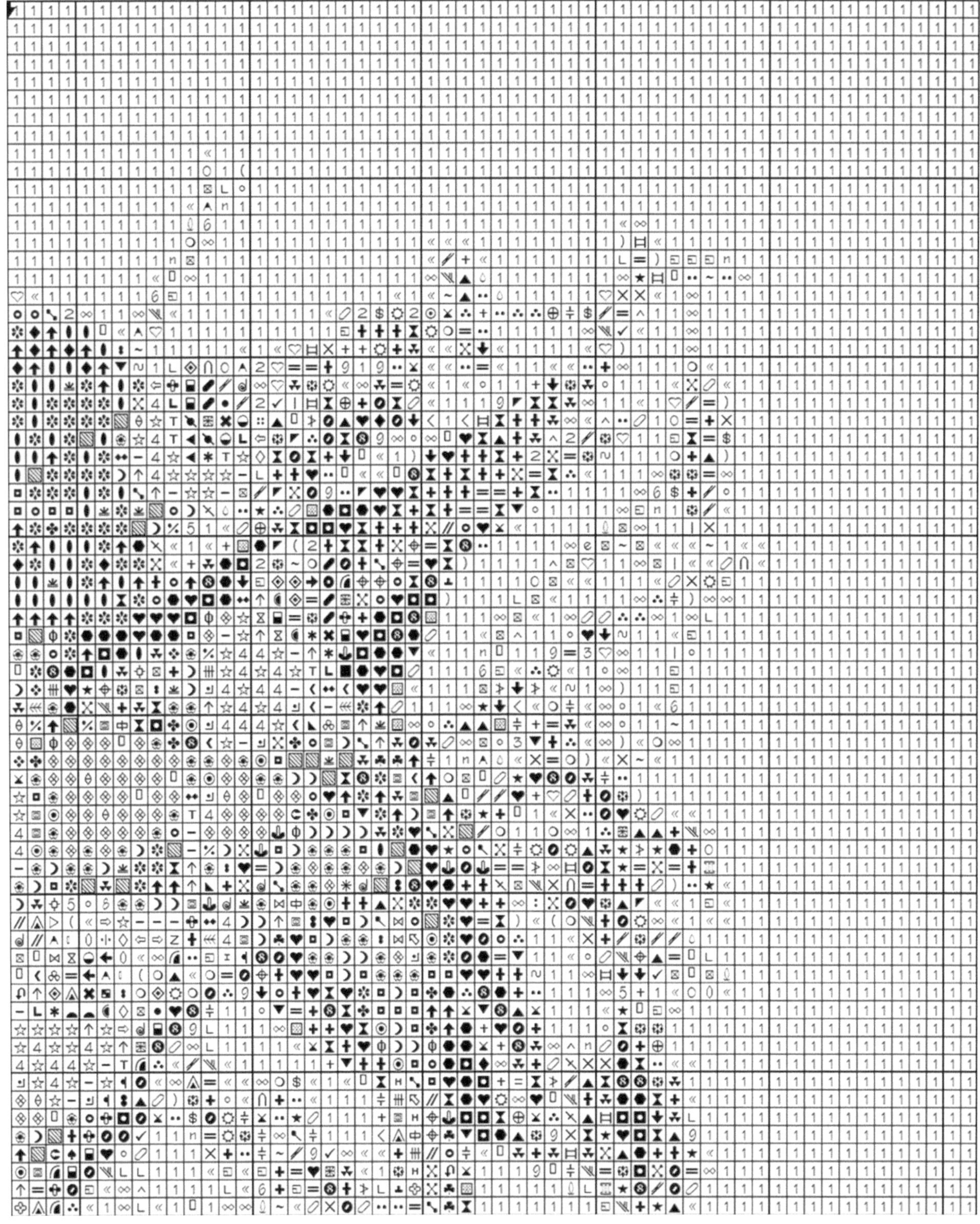

Quadrant 3

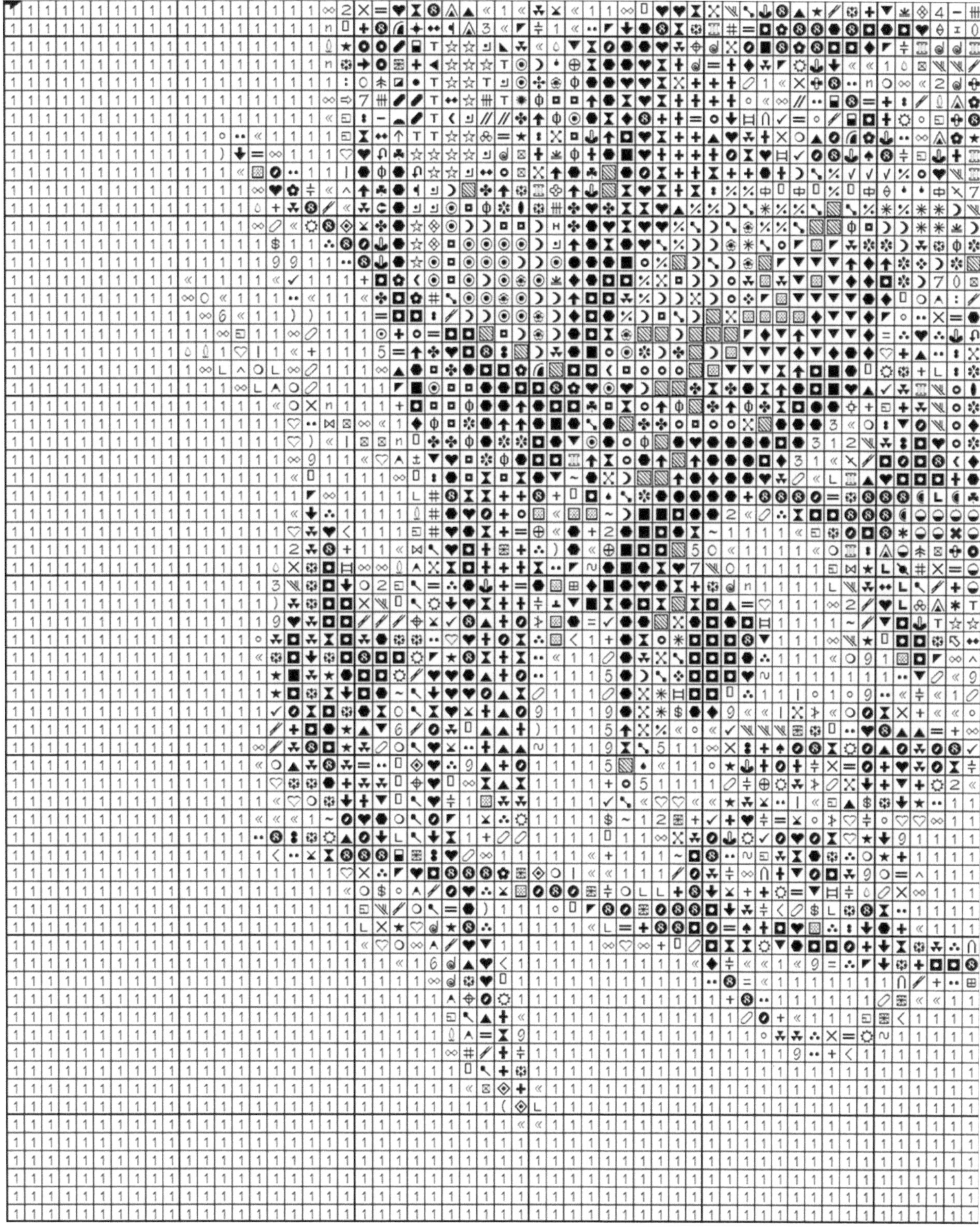

Quadrant 4

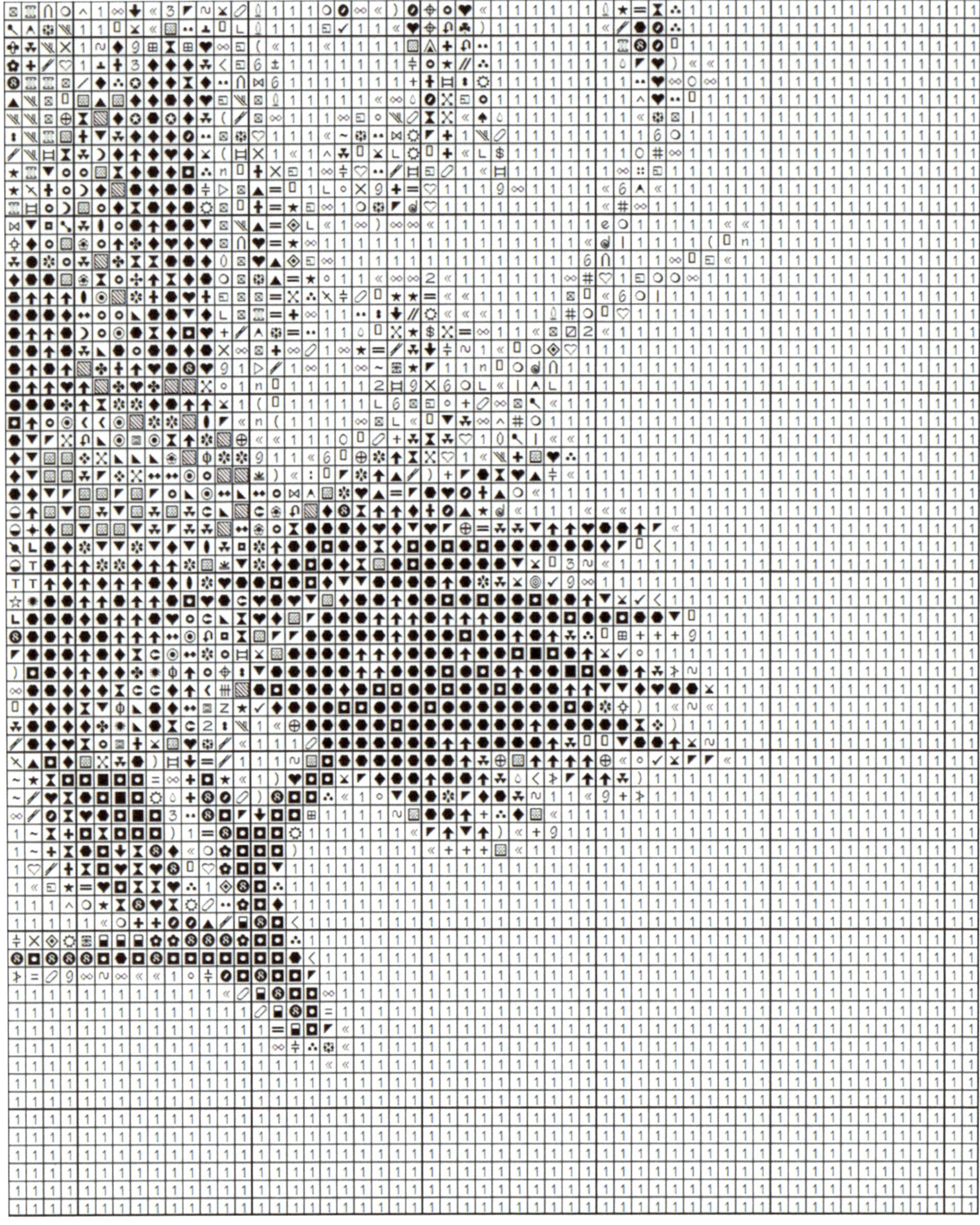

Notes

Notes

Notes

Notes

www.ingramcontent.com/pod-product-compliance
Lightning Source LLC
LaVergne TN
LVHW070209110826
845147LV00002B/548
* 9 7 8 1 6 4 0 0 4 2 7 5 9 *